BRIGHT IDEA BOOKS

SHAPE-SHIFTERS

by Meg Gaertner

Raintree is an imprint of Capstone Global Library Limited, a company incorporated in England and Wales having its registered office at 264 Banbury Road, Oxford, OX2 7DY – Registered company number: 6695582

www.raintree.co.uk
myorders@raintree.co.uk

Edited by Claire Vanden Branden
Designed by Becky Daum
Original illustrations © Capstone Global Library Limited 2021
Production by Colleen McLaren
Originated by Capstone Global Library Ltd

978 1 4747 8768 0 (hardback)
978 1 4747 8778 9 (paperback)

British Library Cataloguing in Publication Data
A full catalogue record for this book is available from the British Library.

Acknowledgements
We would like to thank the following for permission to reproduce photographs: Alamy: Album, 26–27, Erasmus Finx/AF Fotografie, 24; iStockphoto: Callipso, 20–21, lleerogers, 16–17, Lorado, 10–11, mjohnson, 13; Newscom: akg-images/Herbert Kraft, 7, Album/Metropolitan Museum of Art, NY, 9; Shutterstock Images: Bokasana, 19, 28, Brian A Smith, cover (bear), DavidTB, 15, Dean Drobot, cover (man), Nejron Photo, 30–31, Rudmer Zwerver, 5, Tom Tom, cover (forest), Wildlife World, 23. Design Elements: Shutterstock Images, Red Line Editorial.

Printed and bound in India

CONTENTS

CHAPTER ONE
SHAPE-SHIFTERS............. 4

CHAPTER TWO
HUMAN SHAPE-SHIFTING... 8

CHAPTER THREE
LOOKING HUMAN 14

CHAPTER FOUR
SHAPE-SHIFTING GODS 22

Glossary 28
Trivia.................................. 29
Activity 30
Find out more 32
Index.................................. 32

CHAPTER 1

SHAPE-SHIFTERS

A man's body changes. He becomes smaller. His teeth grow sharper. His arms become wings. He was human. Now he is a bat. He is a shape-shifter.

Many **cultures** around the world have **legends** of shape-shifters. These beings can change form. Some are animals that become humans. Some are humans who turn into animals. Others are gods that change form.

In some stories other creatures can be shape-shifters, such as vampires. Many vampires can change into bats.

A LONG HISTORY

Trois Frères is a cave in France. Ancient paintings cover the walls. Many images are 14,000 years old. Some images show strange creatures. They are half human and half animal. Early humans may have believed in shape-shifters. Over time each culture told its own stories.

One drawing in the Trois Frères cave might show a person dressed as a goat.

CHAPTER 2

HUMAN
Shape-shifting

Many stories tell of people turning into animals. Sometimes people change by choice, but sometimes they are **cursed**. Many **fairy tales** describe these curses. One story tells of a prince who turns into a frog. A prince turns into a beast in another story. These curses are often broken by love.

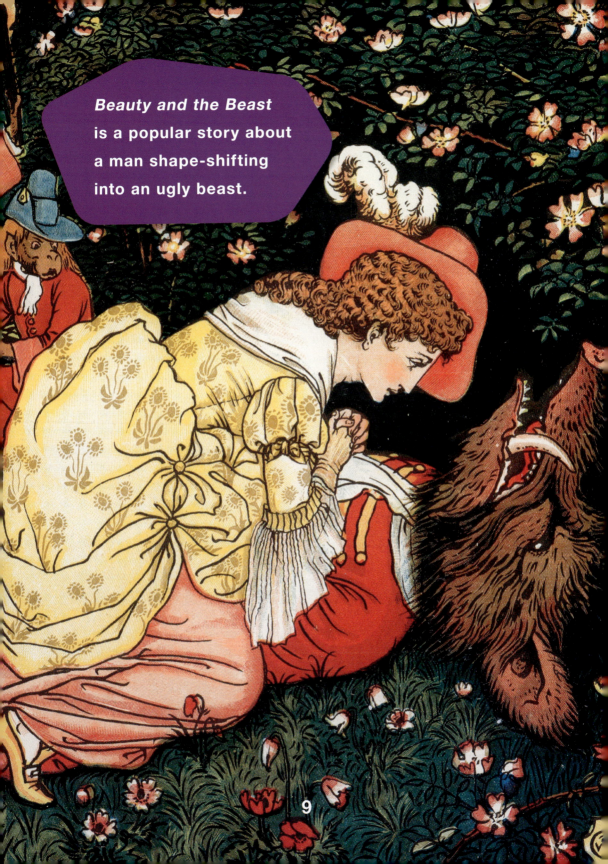

Beauty and the Beast is a popular story about a man shape-shifting into an ugly beast.

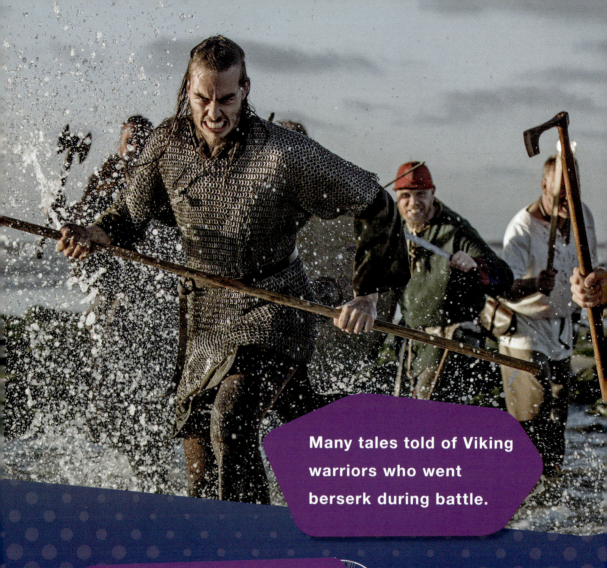

Many tales told of Viking warriors who went berserk during battle.

WEREWOLVES

Many stories talk about werewolves. These are people who turn into wolves. Some can change by choice. Others change during a full moon.

BERSERKERS

In some stories shape-shifters use their power to kill. A **Norse myth** describes the berserkers. These men were strong fighters. They wore wolf or bearskins. They went into a trance in battle. They went out of control (berserk). Some stories say they turned into wolves or bears. They killed many people. The first werewolf stories may have come from the berserkers.

SKINWALKERS

The Navajo people talk about skinwalkers. These are healers who have become evil. They can become coyotes, foxes or wolves. Sometimes they become crows or owls. They can become any animal they want.

Skinwalkers try to hurt or scare people. There is one way to get rid of them. People can find a skinwalker's real name. Then they speak that name out loud. The skinwalker will die or get sick.

Stories say skinwalkers can become foxes.

13

CHAPTER 3

LOOKING
Human

Many cultures describe shape-shifting creatures. These beings can **transform** into humans. They often do this to cause trouble, but sometimes they transform into humans for love.

In some stories people can transform into cats.

SELKIES

Irish and Scottish myths talk about selkies. They swim in the ocean as seals. Then they come onto land. They take off their sealskin. Suddenly the selkies look human. They must put on their skin to return to the sea.

There are stories of humans trapping selkies. A human man takes the skin of a selkie woman. She cannot return to the sea. She becomes the man's wife. Years later she finds her skin. She leaves the man for the ocean.

In many stories, selkies spend most of their time in water. The time they can spend on land willingly may be limited.

DOLPHIN SHAPE-SHIFTERS

Pink river dolphins swim in the Amazon River. One myth says they turn into men at night to kidnap people. They take the people to an underwater city.

KITSUNE

Japanese **folklore** describes the kitsune. It is a Japanese fox demon. It tricks people by looking human. Sometimes it appears helpless. A person stops to help. The kitsune steals from that person. But a kitsune does not always play tricks. It can be thankful when people help it.

Sometimes the kitsune appears as a beautiful lady. It marries a human man. Many stories say the kitsune can create **illusions**. It makes people see things that are not there.

According to Japanese folklore, kitsune are very clever and creative.

STAYING SAFE

Kitsune cannot always hide their tails. Their tails may appear in the mirror. This shows what they really are.

POOKA

Irish stories tell of the pooka. They are goblins. They play tricks on people. Pooka can take many forms. They can become dogs or goats. They can look like rabbits or old men.

Usually a pooka looks like a dark horse with bright eyes. It will invite someone to ride on its back. Then it will scare its rider. It will run fast and make big leaps. The rider will fall off.

Stories of the pooka still exist in Ireland today.

CHAPTER 4

SHAPE-SHIFTING
Gods

Some ancient peoples believed in shape-shifting gods. Zeus was the leader of the ancient Greek gods. He often turned into animals. He used these forms to meet women.

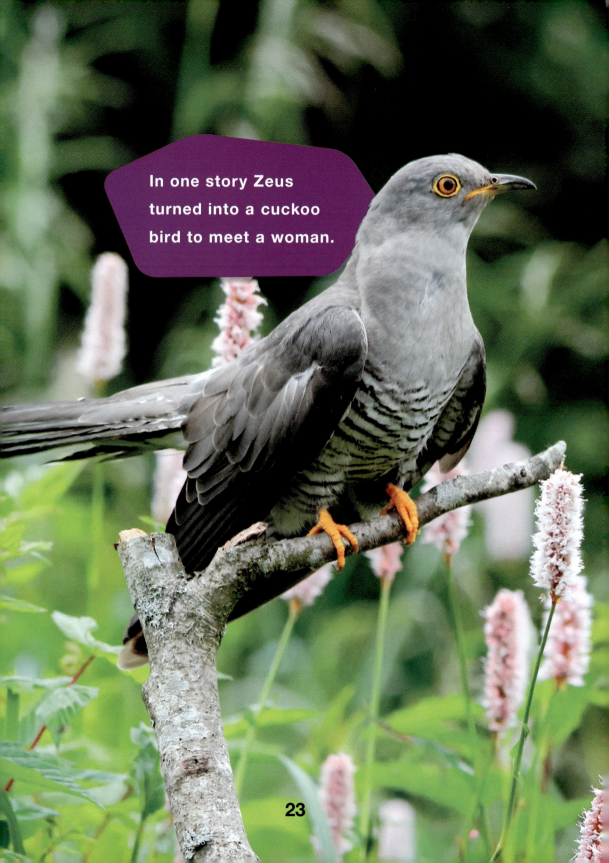

In one story Zeus turned into a cuckoo bird to meet a woman.

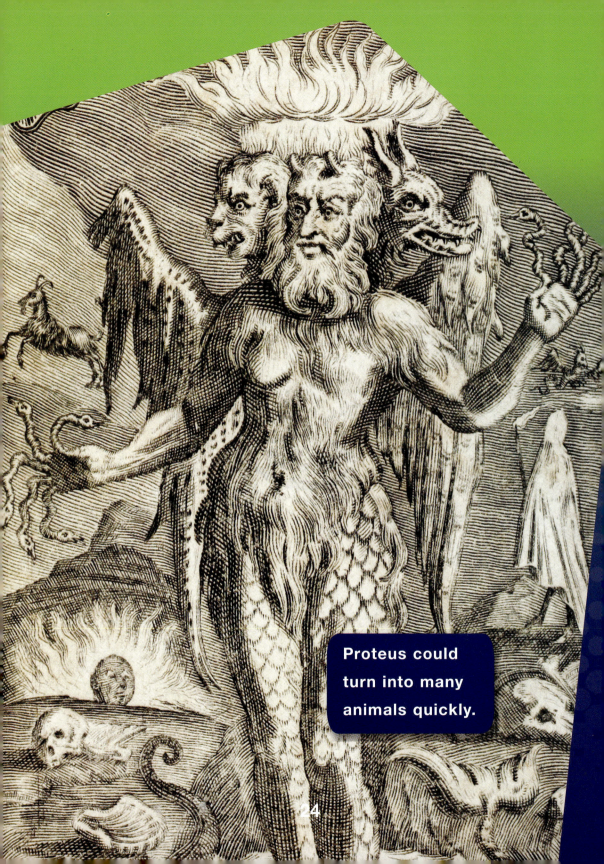

Proteus could turn into many animals quickly.

Proteus was a sea god. He was a wise old man. Many people came to him. They wanted to know the future. They tried to catch him. But Proteus would escape. He changed into many animals to get away.

NORSE GODS

Loki was the Norse god of mischief. He could change his form. He used his shape-shifting to trick people. Odin was another Norse god. He could turn into an eagle.

GLOSSARY

culture
set of beliefs and rules
followed by a group of people

curse
evil spell

fairy tale
children's story about magical
creatures

folklore
stories and beliefs passed
down from generation to
generation in a community

illusion
something that appears to be
real but is not actually real

legend
story that people say is true
but that is not fully based
on fact

myth
story told by people in ancient
times; myths often tried to
explain natural events

Norse
relating to the people or
language of medieval
Scandinavia

transform
make a big change in form
or looks

TRIVIA

1. One legend from the Philippines talks of the Aswang. This creature is a mix between a vampire and a witch. It appears human during the day. It can turn into a deadly dog or beast at night.

2. The Slavs lived in Eastern Europe in ancient times. Their stories spoke of the leshy. This forest creature can appear in many forms. It can look like an old man. It can turn into a plant or animal. A leshy is a trickster. It makes people get lost in the forest.

3. The Algonquins are from Eastern Canada. One of their beliefs speaks of the wiitiko. In some stories it is a spirit that takes over humans. In other stories humans become the wiitiko if they eat other humans. A wiitiko is driven to eat human flesh.

ACTIVITY

WRITE A MYTH

Ancient cultures told stories about their history or beliefs. Many of these stories involved shape-shifters. Write a myth about a shape-shifter. Is your being a human or a creature? What does your being turn into and why? Then draw pictures of your creature in its different forms. Share your story and drawings with family and friends.

FIND OUT MORE

Books

American Indian Stories and Legends (All About Myths), Catherine Chambers (Raintree, 2019)

Myths, Legends and Sacred Stories: A Children's Encyclopedia, DK (DK Children, 2019)

Norse Myths (Mythology Around the World), Eric Braun (Raintree, 2018)

Werewolves: The Truth Behind History's Scariest Shape-shifters (Monster Handbooks), Sean McCollum (Raintree, 2016)

Websites

www.bbc.co.uk/bitesize/topics/zx339j6/articles/ztxwsrd
What is a myth? Find out more!

www.bbc.co.uk/cbbc/quizzes/aotp-asian-mythology-quiz
Which mythical creature are you? Take the quiz to find out!

INDEX

animals 5, 6, 8, 12, 22, 25

berserkers 11

cultures 5, 6, 14

gods 5, 22, 25, 26

kitsune 18, 19

Loki 26

Navajo people 12

Odin 26

pink river dolphins 17

pooka 20

Proteus 25

selkies 16

skinwalkers 12

Trois Frères cave 6

werewolves 10, 11

Zeus 22